D0346826

CONTENTS

Newhailes – the house and estate

Shell Grotto: probably the best surviving example of an eighteenth-century shell-house in Scotland, this distinctive structure was once encrusted with shells and sparkling minerals

Tea House: used by the family to entertain guests. A sketch of the Tea House (detail above) shows it once included a balustrade on both sides, and a large picture window looking up the burn

Earl of Stair's Monument: built to honour John Dalrymple, 2nd Earl of Stair, who, despite accidentally killing his brother in his youth, went on to achieve great military distinction

Stable block: extended into a neo-classical complex by Miss Christian Dalrymple in 1826, these buidings now house interactive displays for visitors, a shop and coffee-house

Sphinx plinths: the lead sphinxes at Newhailes (stolen in 1949) were carefully positioned to draw people out into the landscape. They symbolised wisdom, and the nearby gladiator statues (also vanished) symbolised action, reflecting the Dalrymples' intellectual and military traditions

Ladies' Walk: a unique raised promenade providing a walkway through the Cow and Sheep Parks, to a viewing platform over the Firth of Forth. A favourite with Miss Christian, the walk was intended to elevate the mind as well as, quite literally, the body

Flower Garden: designed to be seen from the Great Apartment of the house, the Flower Garden was once full of interesting fruit trees, vegetables and flowers

'Cabinet Garden': designed as a 'room-within-the-woods', the Cabinet Garden lay just outside the Library and may have been used for study and contemplation

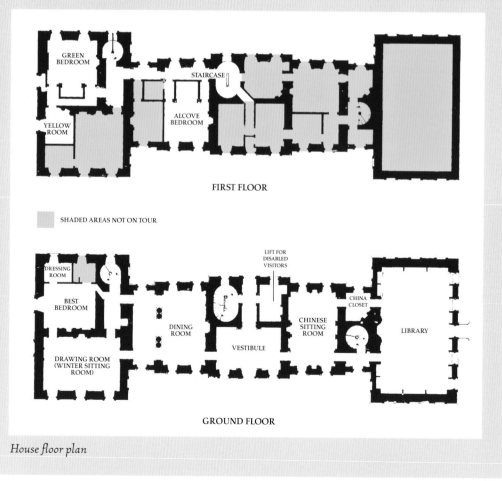

FIRST FLOOR

GREEN BEDROOM

STAIRCASE

YELLOW ROOM

ALCOVE BEDROOM

SHADED AREAS NOT ON TOUR

GROUND FLOOR

DRESSING ROOM

BEST BEDROOM

DINING ROOM

LIFT FOR DISABLED VISITORS

VESTIBULE

CHINESE SITTING ROOM

CHINA CLOSET

LIBRARY

DRAWING ROOM (WINTER SITTING ROOM)

House floor plan

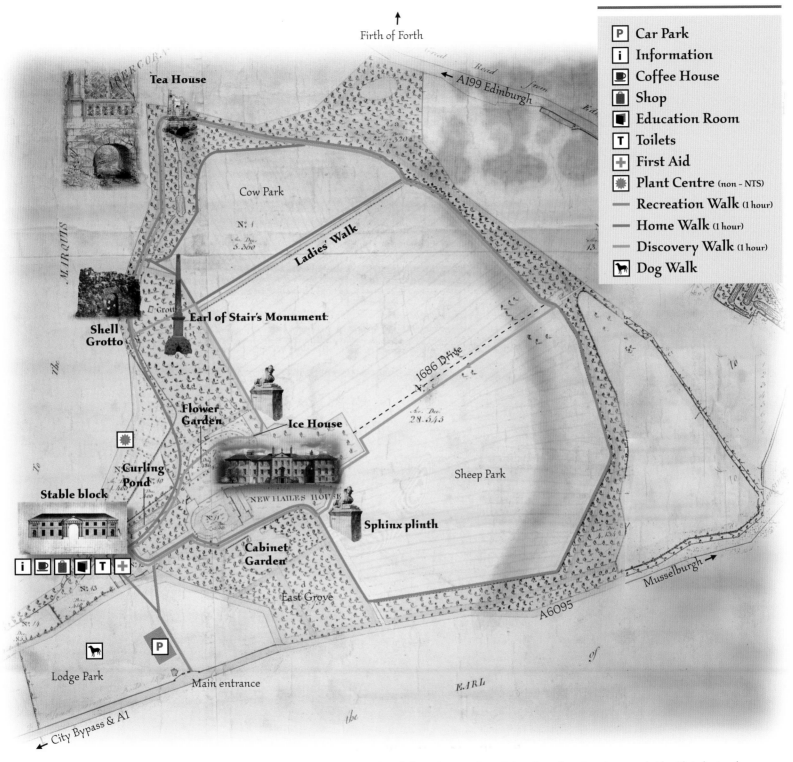

Firth of Forth

Tea House

A199 Edinburgh

Cow Park

Ladies' Walk

Earl of Stair's Monument

Shell
Grotto

1686 Drive

Flower
Garden

Ice House

Sheep Park

Curling
Pond

Stable block

NEW HAILES HOUSE

Sphinx plinth

Cabinet
Garden

Musselburgh

East Grove

A6095

Lodge Park

Main entrance

EARL

City Bypass & A1

P	Car Park
i	Information
⊡	Coffee House
🛍	Shop
⬛	Education Room
T	Toilets
✚	First Aid
✳	Plant Centre (non - NTS)
—	Recreation Walk (1 hour)
—	Home Walk (1 hour)
—	Discovery Walk (1 hour)
🐕	Dog Walk

This map is based on the first dedicated estate plan of 1798, by Robert Bauchop, overlaid with today's references.
♿ *The Recreation Walk is all-ability as far as the Shell Grotto. All other paths require all-terrain wheelchairs.*

Introduction

From the moment you pass through the gateway at **Newhailes**, you are in one of the most intriguing properties in the care of **The National Trust for Scotland**. This fascinating, multi-layered house and historical landscape took centuries to evolve and still remain remarkably complete.

Newhailes was home from 1709 to the influential **Dalrymple** dynasty, who gave the house its important Library and its superb interiors, and created its intricate designed landscape. But almost three centuries later, its existence was threatened. The family, aware of the significance of their home, were determined to keep it intact despite the increasing burdens of taxation, repairs and maintenance. The estate trustees urged The National Trust for Scotland to save the house and estate, primarily to prevent the dispersal of an outstanding collection of works of art from their original setting. With the aid of the Heritage Lottery Fund, the National Art Collections Fund and private donations, the Trust finally succeeded in acquiring Newhailes in 1997.

Historical research and survey work rapidly highlighted and confirmed the significance of the house, where much of the original structure and decoration survive, combining with later additions to produce a unique, complex and mellow character. Research is still proceeding on the no less impressive eighteenth- and nineteenth-century designed landscape which, of its nature, is taking longer to reveal its secrets, but retains much evidence of its original appearance and of its development.

The Trust has respected the untouched character of the house and its immediate surroundings by adopting an innovative conservation strategy. We have carried out as much work as necessary, but as little as possible, to maintain them in a good state of repair while respecting the multi-faceted character of the place that has built up over centuries. We have not restored Newhailes to reflect artificially one single period of its history.

We have carried out as much work as necessary,

but as little as possible

The Men and Women who made Newhailes

The estate, then known as Whitehill, was purchased in 1686 by **James Smith** (1645-1731), described by Colen Campbell in his *Vitruvius Britannicus* (1717) as '***the most experienced architect***' in Scotland. He designed the original house, which now forms the seven central bays of the building, and probably began work on the landscape. Smith had seen the work of the classically-inspired Venetian architect Andrea Palladio, while studying for the priesthood at the Scots College in Rome. His design for the house reflected Palladio's influence, and Newhailes is important as a precursor of the kind of Palladian villa that was later popular throughout Britain, Ireland and North America.

The visitor to Newhailes can compare it with the other buildings by Smith that still survive – the Canongate Church on Edinburgh's Royal Mile, Melville House in Fife and Dalkeith House, Midlothian. He also designed Hamilton Palace, but that is now no longer standing.

In the late seventeenth and early eighteenth century 'villas' like Newhailes were in demand. Edinburgh's lawyers and merchants, whose business affairs required that they lived mainly in the city, also wanted the seclusion of a rural retreat. Smith may, therefore, have built the house as a profitable speculation — but he may equally well have lived there himself, with his large family (from his two marriages he is said to have fathered 32 children — evidently he was not suited for the priesthood!). However, by 1702 Smith had got into financial difficulties after the failure of a mining investment, and he was forced to sell. Seven years later, the estate had been acquired by Sir David Dalrymple for the sum of 40,000 merks (£27,000 — approximately £2.5 million today). Sir David renamed it '**New Hailes**', to link it with his other estate of Hailes, in East Lothian.

During the long ownership of the Dalrymple family the house underwent major development but without fundamentally altering the style of Smith's original building. Remarkably, much of Smith's original building remained intact. The Dalrymples also lavished attention on the surrounding estate, creating over the course of the eighteenth and early nineteenth centuries a perfectly integrated house and designed landscape. The section on the designed landscape (pages 46 to 57) and the map on page 3 of this book will help you discover the secrets of the landscape.

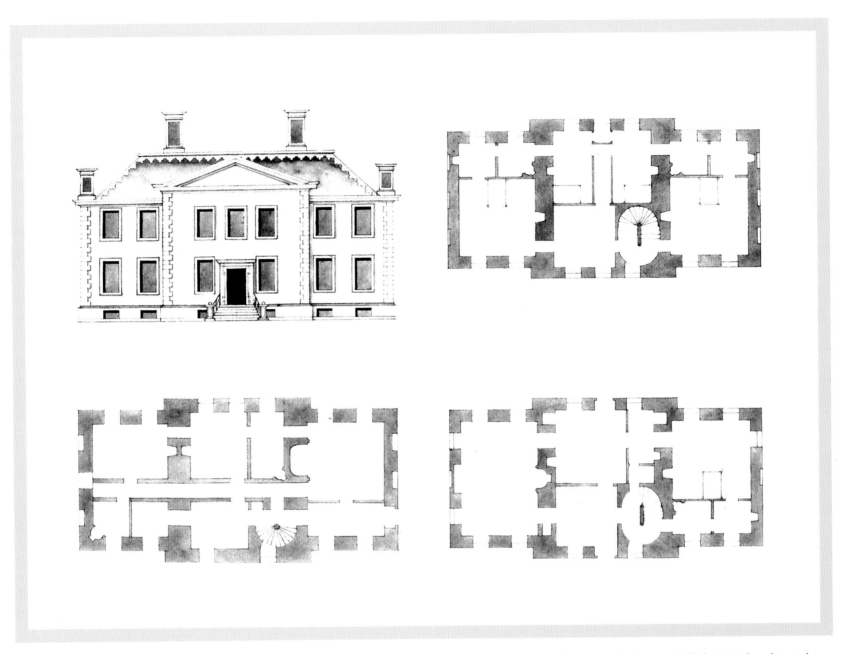

James Smith's plan of the house, 1686. This was found in 1966, alongside many other designs by Smith, among the papers of Colen Campbell, the Scottish architect who played a leading role in the Palladian Revival in England. It seems likely that Smith had acted as mentor to the younger architect.

'...the most experienced architect' in Scotland

The Men and Women who made Newhailes

1645–1731 James Smith. Acquired the estate of Whitehill in 1686 from John Preston.

Surveyor to the Royal Works, a prestigious post bringing important commissions.

Married Janet, daughter of Robert Mylne, Master Mason to the Queen.

Built the original house, but was forced to sell Whitehill when a mining investment failed and his government salary ceased.

c1665–1721 Sir David Dalrymple, 1st Baronet of Hailes. Bought Whitehill in 1709 from Lord Bellenden and renamed it New Hailes.

Solicitor General for Scotland, Lord Advocate, Auditor General of Exchequer.

Married Janet, daughter of Sir James Rochead.

Began work immediately on the Library Wing and developed designed landscape.

1692–1751 Sir James Dalrymple, 2nd Baronet of Hailes. Inherited in 1721.

MP for Haddington, Auditor General of Exchequer.

Married Christian, daughter of Earl of Haddington.

Completed work on Library Wing and built Great Apartment Wing. Changed main entrance of house from north to south. Commissioned and was involved in design of much of the decorative work in the house, which still survives.

Continued his father's landscaping work. Installed sphinxes and gladiator statues.

1800–49 Sir Charles Dalrymple Fergusson, 5th Baronet of Kilkerran (nephew of Miss Christian, grandson of Sir David and his second wife, Helen). Inherited in 1838.

Advocate and diplomat.

Married Helen, daughter of Rt Hon David Boyle, Lord Justice General.

Ordered sale of over 500 trees. Continued disputes with railway owners.

1839–1916 Sir Charles Dalrymple, 1st Baronet of Newhailes (younger son of Sir Charles Dalrymple Fergusson). Inherited in 1849, at the age of ten (Sir Charles's eldest son inherited the Fergusson Kilkerran estate).

Privy Councillor, Conservative MP for Buteshire and for Ipswich, junior Lord of the Treasury.

Married Alice Mary Hunter Blair (died in childbirth 1884).

Took local responsibilities seriously and active in community: Newhailes used for local events.

1828–1904 Alexander, Baron Shand of Woodhouse. Leased Newhailes 1873–83.

Scottish judge and First Lord of Appeal.

Married Emily Merelina Meymott.

Many improvements carried out to house, in agreement with Sir Charles Dalrymple, including installation of gas supply and plumbing improvements. Larger panes of plate glass installed in windows on principal floor.

New greenhouses erected.

1726–92 Sir David Dalrymple, 3rd Baronet, Lord Hailes. Inherited in 1751.

Lord of Justiciary, respected historian.

Married first, Anne Broun and second, Helen, daughter of Sir James Fergusson, 2nd Baronet, Lord Kilkerran (of the Kilkerran estate in Ayrshire). The second marriage created future heirs of Newhailes, and a link between the Dalrymple and Fergusson families that survives to this day.

Developed collection of books in Library, which acquired its outstanding reputation. Commissioned further work on designed landscape, including a start to the building of the Shell Grotto.

1765–1838 Miss Christian Dalrymple (eldest daughter of Sir David). Inherited Newhailes estate in 1792, but not the title.

She never married.

Had Library reroofed, and often used it for entertaining. Improved garrets for servants' accommodation. Added the palace front to the Stable Block. Maintained and developed the designed landscape, especially the Flower Garden. Protected the grounds as far as possible from the effects of industrialisation and railways.

1879–1932 Sir David Dalrymple, 2nd Baronet of Newhailes (son of Sir Charles Dalrymple). Inherited in 1916. Lieutenant in Royal Navy. Never lived at Newhailes.

Married Margaret MacTaggart-Stewart (divorced 1919).

1915–71 Sir Mark Dalrymple, 3rd Baronet of Newhailes (son of Sir David Dalrymple). Inherited in 1932, and died without heir. Lady Antonia, Sir Mark's widow, continued to live in the house, and the estate was administered by trustees. Much of estate and associated buildings let out to provide revenue for repairs to house.

(Lady Antonia continues to live on the estate.)

1997 Newhailes acquired by **The National Trust for Scotland**.

2002 The house and new Stables Visitor Centre opened to the public, after a five-year conservation project, at a ceremony attended by HRH Prince Charles.

Sir James, 1st Viscount Stair, by Sir John de Medina

Sir John, 1st Earl of Stair, 2nd Viscount, also by de Medina

Sir David, 1st Baronet of Hailes, by Sir Godfrey Kneller

The Dalrymples

The Dalrymples were an influential dynasty of lawyers and politicians who dominated the Scottish legal system at a crucial stage in its history. **Sir David Dalrymple**, who bought Newhailes, was the fifth son of the **1st Viscount Stair**, a prominent judge and author of the influential *Institutions of Scottish Law* (published in 1681). Stair was for a time the king's ambassador to France, and passed on to his children the sophisticated artistic tastes he acquired at the court of Louis XIV.

Sir David's older brother, **John, 1st Earl of Stair**, held the offices of Lord Justice Clerk, Lord Advocate and Secretary of State. In this capacity, he authorised government troops to slaughter members of the Jacobite MacDonald clan in Glencoe in 1692.

Sir David himself occupied a succession of well-paid government posts that enabled him to fund the enhancement of Newhailes, his rural retreat. A Member of Parliament from 1698 to 1721, he represented first Culross (in the Scottish Parliament), then Haddington (in the first united parliament at Westminster). In 1701 he was made 1st Baronet of Hailes and Solicitor General for Scotland, a post that he held until his appointment as Lord Advocate in 1709. Sir David was also a Commissioner for the Union of the Scottish and English parliaments in 1706, Auditor General of the Exchequer (1720-1) and Dean of the Faculty of Advocates from 1712 until his death in 1721. He was closely involved in the expansion of the Advocates' Library in Edinburgh, and clearly brought this passion for books to his plans for Newhailes.

The prominence and scale of the Library that Sir David had built on the principal floor, at a time when most domestic libraries were tucked away on the upper floors, and could hardly muster a shelf-ful of books, was then almost certainly unique in Scotland. It suggests that Sir David already possessed an impressive collection of books.

Sir James Dalrymple (1692-1751) succeeded his father both as MP for Haddington and as the Auditor General of the Exchequer. Like many young British aristocrats, he completed his education with a 'Grand Tour' of Europe in 1708, and the classical (and neo-classical) architecture he saw in Italy may have influenced his ideas for developing the Newhailes library, as well as the 'pleasure grounds' surrounding the house. Sir James and his wife, **Lady Christian**, also built the Great Apartment (1728-33) with its superb rococo interiors.

There is a Book, called 'Flagellum or the Life of Oliver Cromwell,' which I have commissioned for the Library; but as it is a very scarce Book, & these Commissions are not soon answered, I may wait long before I get it. I know you have a very large Library; and if that Book be in it, I shall be very much obliged to you for a Loan of it; that being now the Period, which I have begun upon. I am

Edinr. 3d of April
1754

Sir
Your most obedient Servant
David Hume

Their heir was **Sir David Dalrymple, Lord Hailes** (1726-92). Appointed a Lord of Justiciary in 1776, Lord Hailes was a prominent figure in the age of the Scottish Enlightenment. One of the foremost Scottish historians and antiquaries of the period, he is likely to have entertained at Newhailes some of the major figures of contemporary Scottish intellectual history. His papers include correspondence with key Enlightenment figures such as philosopher David Hume, historian William Robertson, playwright John Home, economist and philosopher Adam Smith and judge and philosopher Henry Home, Lord Kames.

It was during this time that the Library gained its great reputation. It is easy to imagine Lord Hailes writing many of his books in this inspiring room, including his most important, the *Annals of Scotland*. Dr Samuel Johnson revised the manuscript of this book and, according to family tradition, described the Newhailes Library as '**the most learned drawing room in Europe**' — though this interesting observation has never been verified.

Lord Hailes died in 1792 with no male heir, and Newhailes was inherited by his daughter, **Christian Dalrymple** (1765-1838), although the title passed to her cousin, **James Dalrymple Fergusson**. Her descendant, Hew Dalrymple, commented when he published Miss Christian's *Private Annals* in 1914: '**The story I have heard was that Lord Hailes's will could not be found and that they were preparing to leave Newhailes when the will was found behind a shutter**' (it is not clear whether the shutter was at Newhailes or in Lord Hailes's house in New Street, Edinburgh). Although she did not expect to inherit, estate records and Miss Christian's own diaries show that she devoted at least as much attention to the house and its surroundings as the previous three generations of owners.

Miss Christian and the unexpected inheritance

Miss Christian Dalrymple's Journals of 1798-1838 are in the National Library of Scotland, Edinburgh, and are an invaluable source of information about domestic life at the time. She writes of inheriting Newhailes: *'I was informed by Sir A Fergusson that I was the heiress of this estate, instead of being banished from this place which I had expected.'* Despite this unexpected turn of events – it was very unusual for a daughter to inherit property – she devoted much attention to the estate. Even on Christmas Day 1813, she was walking the grounds planning improvements!

We learn from her journals how she runs a household of servants, dealing with the consequences when they get drunk, get married secretly and prune favourite trees too ruthlessly.

She also records trips to the theatre (once to see the famous Mrs Siddons in **Hamlet**) and to municipal firework displays to mark a royal event or a victory over Napoleon. She is thrilled to witness the famous visit of George IV to Edinburgh in 1822, masterminded by Sir Walter Scott.

And sometimes the brutality of life intrudes into her conscientiously ordered world. A starving man is found near the gate, and she orders him to be fed; a poacher is caught in the grounds, and dispatched to the Musselburgh tollbooth; the hen house is robbed; and disease is rife. She writes in early 1832: *'January 19, Cholera appeared in Musselburgh. February 3, was put in a great Flutter by hearing one of the sons of Mr Mitchell had died of Cholera, this greatly increased my panic as it showed the disease was attacking a different Class.'*

Miss Christian's most significant improvements to the house were the reroofing of the Library and the division of the attic garrets for staff accommodation, for which she commissioned the renowned architect James Gillespie Graham. She wrote with satisfaction in her diary on 9 October 1816: *'Went all over the House to see the Improvements on the Garrets which are now rooms fit for anyone to inhabit.'* She also extended the Stable Block, and devoted much energy to the designed landscape, carefully maintaining established features but also adding embellishments such as the formal Flower Garden. Under her stewardship the integrity of the whole estate was respected — for the last time, as it turned out. Subsequent owners in the nineteenth and early twentieth centuries had their chief estates elsewhere; Newhailes became less of a family home and parts of the house and grounds were leased off to tenants.

Above: seedsman's bill, 1831

Below: architect's drawing for 1826 extension of the Stable Block

Background image: John Hay's plan for the Flower Garden, commissioned in 1818 by Miss Christian

Christian's nephew **Sir Charles Dalrymple Fergusson**, the only grandson of Lord Hailes, inherited the estate after the death of his aunt in 1838, of which he wrote poignantly: '*I have lost a Parent, a Friend, an affectionate, disinterested, faithful, judicious Advisor, whose frequent councils I too often slighted and was impatient of*'. During his ownership the house, coach house and stables were let at an annual rent of £200, and the family lived here only sporadically. Sir Charles travelled extensively but was also very much engaged in 'good works' in the local community. His papers show a keen involvement in the Edinburgh Charity Workhouse from 1827 to 1835 and in the opening of a Fishermen's School at nearby Fisherrow.

FISHERMEN'S SCHOOL.

The SCHOOL in the Back of Fisherrow, intended exclusively for the accommodation of the Children of FISHERMEN in Northesk Parish, will be opened on Monday next, the 9th Instant, at 10 o'Clock, Fore-noon, under the superintendence of Mr A. H. LAMB.

It is earnestly hoped that this School will be taken advantage of by Fishermen for the Education of their Children.

FEES:—

For Reading, ... 2d. per week.
For Reading and Writing, . . . 2½d. do.
For Reading, Writing and Arithmetic, 3d. do.

Northesk, 5th May 1842.

Charles's widow and seven children, attended by sixteen servants, lived here after his death in 1849, when the estate was inherited by his son, Sir Charles Dalrymple. Sir Charles entered parliament as Conservative MP for Buteshire in 1868 and represented the county until 1885, when he unsuccessfully contested the Midlothian constituency against Gladstone. He was Grand Master Mason of Scotland from 1894 to 1896.

Charles's political career obliged him to keep houses in London and on the Isle of Bute. Until 1883, when he was able to return to Newhailes to live, he leased the estate to Edinburgh-based professionals who found the railway link with the capital enormously convenient. Between 1849 and 1873 the tenant was Henry Coventry. From 1873, Newhailes was leased to **Alexander, Baron Shand of Woodhouse**, a prominent Edinburgh lawyer, for a term of ten years, at an annual rent of £250.

Before he took up the lease, Lord Shand insisted on a significant programme of repairs and improvements. This included the removal of the glazing bars to the windows in the main rooms on the principal floor and the installation of fashionable plate glass, whose rather stark appearance was offset by window boxes and by creepers cultivated to drape across the façade. Gas pipes and fittings were installed throughout the house, and in November 1873 Sir Charles wrote that Lord Shand '*had the gas lighted in all the rooms and showed me thro' the house which is very bright and comfortable*'. Central heating was introduced, the bell-and-wire system for summoning servants was upgraded and new bathrooms were put in. A new fresh water supply was plumbed in – despite this, however, the house was hit by an outbreak of typhoid in 1882, and the Shands decamped to a hotel while remedial work was carried out on the water mains.

Below: Sir Charles Dalrymple Fergusson was chargé d'affaires for the British government in Switzerland. This laissez-passer document for Sir Charles, 'gentilhomme anglais', was issued to assure his safe passage in Italy

Bottom: Sir Charles Dalrymple (right) photographed at the entrance to the house between 1903 and 1906, with Joseph Chamberlain, former leader of the Liberal Unionists, Secretary for the Colonies and father of the future Prime Minister, Neville Chamberlain

Far left: Sir Alexander
Burns Shand,
1st Baron Shand, by Sir
Leslie Ward ('Spy')

Left: Emily Merelina
Meymott, Baroness Shand,
by Robert Herdman

Sir Charles Dalrymple's diaries and correspondence, also in the National Library of Scotland, provide fascinating insights into contemporary public affairs and politics: but also include deeply personal reflections, including a poignant account of the death in childbirth of his wife at Newhailes, in 1884. The baby girl survived and was named Alice Mary after her mother. Charles was left to bring up the three children alone, and felt the loss of his wife keenly for many years.

'August 31, 1890: My little child's sixth birthday falls on a Sunday, as the date of her birth did in 1884. The memories of that grievous time are very fresh .... God has been gracious to me and to my dear children. And we have had the help and sympathy of many ... Our dear one is at rest in Him ... I earnestly hope to be enabled to do my duty by our dear children, who have many of her qualities of head and heart.'

The young Alice Mary returned her father's devotion, as shown by the many lively letters to him in the archive. She particularly liked the time she spent at Newhailes:

'4 June 1903: Yesterday was a beautiful day. I visited the garden and rock garden and Mary F and I walked along the terrace toward the Shell House in the morning and Dickie and I walked towards Parkend, along the grass walk above the Catherine Bower where the may blossom is lovely.'

Alice Mary in the garden, 1906

Lord Shand also required improvements to the surrounding estate and to garden buildings, such as the hot-houses. One of his letters requests repairs to the fence to keep the sheep off the lawn, so that they would not **'zoom all over the grounds'** and devour his Virginia creeper.

The Shands were sensitive to the importance of the superb eighteenth-century interiors at Newhailes and, probably at the insistence of Charles Dalrymple, repainted rooms in the same colour schemes that had been adopted in the early eighteenth century. This period in art and architecture was beginning to become fashionable again, and it is largely thanks to the Shands' tastes that these interiors have survived so well.

In 1874 Sir Charles consolidated the family's Ayrshire connections by marrying Alice Mary, from the well-known Hunter Blair family of Ayr. The Shands offered to break the lease to allow the young couple to take up residence, but it was not until 1883 that the Dalrymples once more returned to live at Newhailes. Sir Charles wrote in his diary: **'It is a wonderful thing that we should find ourselves back at the old home after an absence of nine years.'**

During Charles's lifetime the house and the estate were well maintained. He took a great interest in local affairs: on the occasion of Queen Victoria's Diamond Jubilee in 1897, he made over a field on the Newhailes estate to the local people a decision prompted by the escape from drowning of his only son. 'I hope', he wrote, **'that the field may be a source of pleasure to the people of Newcraighall, and that all will unite in so using it that its natural beauty may be preserved for the benefit and enjoyment of all'.** The field is now used by the Niddrie Bowling Club. Under Sir Charles's ownership, Newhailes was often the focus of community events, including annual outings for local schoolchildren.

Sir Charles's only son, David, was only five when his mother died, and he never had a settled family life nor formed a lasting attachment to Newhailes. He served as a Lieutenant in the Royal Navy, and rarely came home even on leave. In 1906 David married Margaret Anna, the youngest of Sir Mark MacTaggart-Stewart's daughters, who were all celebrated beauties. In 1915 she gave birth to a son, christened Mark after his grandfather.

Sir David succeeded to the Newhailes estate on the death of his father in 1916. His marriage ended in divorce in 1919, and as a consequence he ran into financial difficulties. Mark was brought up by his mother in the south of England, but always felt a deep love for Newhailes: there is a story of his having been given some chocolate gold coins as a child, and announcing: '**Look, Mummy, money – we don't have to leave Newhailes**'. Trustees for Mark — who inherited at the age of 17 when his father died — took over the running of the estate, and let it to his mother's sister and her husband, the Earl and Countess of Cassillis. The Earl was heir to the Marquess of Ailsa, whose seat was Culzean Castle, but he needed a home near Edinburgh since he practised as an advocate.

He and his wife carried out a sensitive programme of repairs to the house, at a time when it would otherwise have suffered neglect. They lived there until Sir Mark came of age in 1936, but the outbreak of World War II a few years later claimed him for service in the radar section of the Royal Air Force and his mother, now remarried to Sir Patrick Blake, '**held the fort**' (as she put it) for him at his beloved Newhailes.

In 1946 **Sir Mark** married **Lady Antonia Stewart**, daughter of the Earl of Galloway, and the couple at last set up house at Newhailes, creating a comfortable flat on the first floor of the house — including Miss Christian's bedroom. Sir Mark extended sand quarrying on the estate (which remained active until the 1970s), and housing development took place in the North Park. The estate as a whole suffered from the shortage of available labour after World War II, and much of the land and the estate buildings were leased to raise money for a continual programme of repairs and maintenance to the house. From 1948 to 1978 a very successful mink farm operated here, and a market garden, followed by a plant centre, took over the old walled garden. It is now the Newhailes Nursery.

Sir Mark and Lady Antonia never had any children and, after his sudden death in 1971, the management of Newhailes was taken on by a group of trustees on behalf of Lady Antonia, who continued to live in the house, sometimes sharing it with art student lodgers, whose rent enabled her to stay on. She was determined to keep Newhailes going at all costs, and sometimes conducted tours for learned societies — but she was increasingly haunted by the prospect of, in her words, '**an auction on the lawn**' of the precious contents, due to the enormous cost of maintaining the estate.

In 1997 the trustees gifted the house and policies into the care of The National Trust for Scotland, who purchased the contents of the house from Lady Antonia with the help of the funding bodies acknowledged inside the front cover of this book.

The edifying inscriptions

The Latin inscription over the main door, '*Laudo manentem*,' is taken from an ode by Horace, the great Roman poet, and means '*I praise her while she stays*'. The poet is lamenting the fickle nature of Fate, but resigns himself to enjoying her favours while he can. Classically educated visitors to the house in the eighteenth century would have recognised the reference. The motto could also mean '*I praise those who stay here*,' and so is very suitable as a welcoming greeting.

The motto engraved at the same level at the back of the house, '*Sapienter uti*,' is also taken from Horace. It translates as '*Use wisely*,' and comes from an ode that carries the same stoical message as the inscription at the front of the house: '*He ... rightly deserves to be called happy who knows how to use wisely the gifts of the gods*.'

Main door inscription

Rear door inscription

Tour of the House

'*No one familiar with the castles and neo-classic mansions of Scotland can fail to have been impressed with the ravages which were worked on them inside and out during the nineteenth century ... it is the more pleasant, therefore, to be able to illustrate a house which shows the decorative art of the first half of the eighteenth century untouched by the hand of the "restorer".*'
Lawrence Weaver, architectural editor of *Country Life*, writing about Newhailes in 1917.

The Entrance

Visitors enter the house in the same way as they would have done from the 1730s, when the main entrance of the house was changed from the north side to the south, probably to free the then serene parkland and pleasure grounds from the disturbance of carriages coming and going. The shape of the forecourt and the gate piers were copied from Lord Burlington's design for his villa in Chiswick, London.

The stucco doorcase was modelled on Michelangelo's door to the Laurentian Library in Florence. The two profile heads were based on sculpted heads thought in the 1730s to be Roman — they are now believed to be fragments of a sixteenth-century building in Edinburgh's Old Town, and can be seen in the Museum of Scotland. The present oak door with its wrought-iron furniture was supplied by MacGibbon in 1873 and has been carefully repaired by the Trust.

A photograph of 1917 showing the gate piers with their gas lamps

Baroque and Rococo

The shell motif that appears so often at Newhailes was common in the mid-eighteenth-century style of architecture and decoration known as rococo — but the number of times it recurs here is remarkable. Flowers, branches, rustic scenes and fantastical European interpretations of Chinese motifs ('Chinoiserie') were also characteristic of this style. Rococo was a lighter, freer and more playful development of the baroque style in architecture, prevalent in the late seventeenth and early eighteenth centuries, especially in continental Europe. The baroque style delighted in expansive curvaceous forms, large-scale complex compositions and exuberant decoration. In Britain, this style was always tempered by the simpler, cleaner lines of classicism and never reached the heights of the form as practised in Italy, Austria, Germany and Spain.

The Great Apartment at Newhailes is one of the most superb surviving rococo interiors in Britain today. As you walk through the house, you will see many examples of rococo details in the decoration. Note particularly the exquisite ormolu (gilded bronze) door-handles, with their tiny shells that turn to operate the bolt. Such elaborate door-handles are very rare in a comparatively modest British country house like this.

17

The Vestibule

Created from two small rooms of the original villa when the house was turned back-to-front in the 1730s, this space offers breathtaking views across the park and the Firth of Forth. The skill of the Dalrymples' landscape gardeners and a natural raised beach effectively conceal nearby houses, even today.

The Vestibule is decorated with plasterwork by the renowned craftsman **Thomas Clayton**, who charged **Sir James Dalrymple** £44 for this commission in 1742. Its architectural style is typical of Georgian halls, which were regarded as a transition between outdoors and indoors. The austere design is intended to recall the villas of ancient Rome, an effect that is heightened by a set of eight mahogany lobby stools by Nix, a fashionable London cabinetmaker, which resemble the folding bronze stools of antiquity.

Clayton displayed a lighter touch in his frieze, with its delightfully docile lions, their manes ruffled by the breeze. The tassels were probably originally intended to frame family portraits. Over the side doors, the decorative baskets of shells give the visitor the first glimpse of a recurring motif at Newhailes. The shell was a vital component of rococo decoration, but it is not clear why it was so fascinating to the Dalrymple family. It may simply reflect the closeness of the sea, and the fact that Musselburgh was famous for the shell banks that probably gave the town its name.

Clayton displayed a lighter touch in his frieze, with its delightfully docile lions, their manes ruffled by the breeze.

In the late nineteenth century this room was known as the 'Billiard Room', and a photograph taken about 1890 (below) shows the billiard table in place. In 1906 the table was used to display wedding gifts presented to Sir David Dalrymple and his first wife. Souvenirs collected by the couple in the China Seas during Sir David's naval career were later displayed on the shelves installed in 1839. Chinese Chippendale chairs continued this theme – only one of the set still survives. Also here are a superb pair of early eighteenth-century gesso tables, two fine lacquer cabinets and a Regency lacquer worktable.

Textile detail on sofa

Chinese cabinet detail

The Chinese Sitting Room

This was the '**great dining room**' of Smith's original villa. It is the only public room at Newhailes to retain intact its original late seventeenth-century panelling, which survived because the room was subsequently downgraded to an ordinary parlour, where the family took their everyday meals, and so did not need fashionable redecoration. The central recess opposite the fireplace may be the original buffet recess, of the kind used for serving food before sideboards became fashionable. **Sir James Dalrymple** modernised the room by installing, around 1730, a new fireplace in veined grey marble, possibly supplied from the Adam family's marble works in nearby Leith. It still contains its original grate, one of the house's unique collection of early Georgian grates.

Sir James must also have installed the baroque recesses between the windows, topped by ovals and festoons painted in 1739 by James Norie, who carried out most of the documented decorative painting at Newhailes. The survival of such early eighteenth-century *trompe l'oeil* ornamental detail is extremely rare — it has usually been painted over.

Family Portraits

The overdoor portraits of the family were incorporated into the panelling in the early nineteenth century, when this room ceased to be the main dining room. Over the fireplace is a portrait of Sir David, the first Dalrymple owner of Newhailes, by Sir Godfrey Kneller (c1646-1723). Continuing clockwise around the room, next is a portrait by the famous Scottish painter Allan Ramsay (1713-84) of Sir David's grandson, Lord Hailes. Over the door to the Library closet is a portrait attributed to William Aikman (1682-1731) of Sir James Dalrymple. Over the Library door hangs a portrait from the circle of Sir John de Medina (c1655-1710) of Hew Dalrymple, Sir David's brother. Above the entrance door from the Vestibule is a very spirited portrait by Ramsay of Lord Drummore, Sir James's cousin, who was a close neighbour, living in a villa at Cockenzie.

Sir David   Lord Hailes   Hew Dalrymple   Lord Drummore

In 1743 Thomas Clayton was paid £28 for 'ornamenting the Liberarey Chimley Peace at Newhailes in stucco' — presumably to help integrate the ornate polychrome marble chimneypiece into a sober, practical room devoted to study. The monumental chimneypiece must have been one of the first by Italian sculptors imported into Britain, though they later became one of the favourite souvenirs of a young milord's Grand Tour. In a letter of 1730, Sir James refers to ordering a chimneypiece in Rome: another of 1732 expresses his anxiety in case customs officers open it and cause damage.

Below: Clayton's receipt for work on the Library chimneypiece

The Library Wing

The eastern wall of the Chinese Sitting Room marks the end wall of Smith's original villa. The visitor then enters the remarkable Library Wing, added by **Sir David Dalrymple**, and completed around 1722. The sheer scale of this magnificent space cannot fail to impress — Sir David's new wing was almost equal in volume to the whole of Smith's villa, and was built at a time when few people possessed enough books to justify the building of a special room to keep them in.

The wing is raised on vaulted cellars, to protect the books from damp. As well as the Library proper, it contains a closet — now the **China Closet** — and its own spiral service stair off the Library lobby, leading to a small room directly above the closet, probably intended for a legal clerk whose task would be to make fair copies of letters drafted by his employer.

Well lit by its five tall east-facing windows, the Library was clearly built with regard to the recommendation of writers of ancient Greece and Rome that books should be consulted in the morning, with the benefit of light from the east.

The bookshelves are adjustable — a remarkable innovation in the early eighteenth century and more typical of modern libraries — and, by means of an ingenious system of chamfered edges, run right into the corners of the walls. This makes maximum use of the space but also makes it impossible to reach the last half-dozen volumes on each shelf, so these corners were boxed in during the early nineteenth century. Notice how the shelves not only occupy the total height of every wall, but burrow into the spaces around the doors and the chimneypiece. A visitor of 1876 remarked that the Library was, under the Shands' tenancy, '**rather useless, as the bookcases are seventeen feet high, and there is no ladder to reach the upper shelves by**'.

Clayton's fine plasterwork appropriately frames a portrait by Sir John de Medina of **Sir David Dalrymple**, the builder of the Library, with his son **James**, who added the chimneypiece. The pedestal library table was purchased from Sam Smith, London, in 1743 for £15, and the conventional set of stuffed chairs was added by Lord Hailes. He made few changes to this remarkable room, but benefited from its rich resources to become one of the great scholars of the Scottish Enlightenment.

Opposite: photograph of c1930 showing the books in place in the Library

Library,
Newhailes.

23

'This is the historical Nation': the Scottish Enlightenment

Lord Hailes was one of the many scholars, writers and thinkers who contributed to the ferment of intellectual activity in the mid-eighteenth century that became known later as '**the Scottish Enlightenment**'. The birth of this unprecedented spirit of enquiry was stimulated by an enormous growth in trade and commerce. It was also made possible by the decisive defeat in 1746 of the Jacobites, which ushered in a period of relative social peace. The Enlightenment was inspired by, and linked to, contemporary rational thinkers in Continental Europe, including **Jean d'Alembert** and **Denis Diderot** in France. The first volume of their *Encyclopédie*, published in 1751, was hugely influential. It described and defined the natural world in a new way, and was imbued with the conviction that it was possible to know everything and to apply that knowledge usefully. The Enlightenment encouraged further research in the natural and scientific world, heralding almost two centuries of pioneering work by Scottish scientists, doctors, explorers and entrepreneurs.

David Hume (1711–76), by Allan Ramsay

Edinburgh – and to a lesser extent Glasgow and Aberdeen – became centres of debate in a way that London never did, though English scientists and philosophers like Newton and Locke provided great inspiration for thinkers north of the border. Arguably, since the franchise was still much more limited in Scotland, well-educated Scots devoted more of their energies to intellectual pursuits because many were denied the access to politics enjoyed by their English counterparts. The philosopher David Hume, a key Enlightenment figure, expressed how important his contemporaries considered the writing of history and the establishment of their place in it, when he wrote in a letter of 1770:

'**This is the historical Age and this the historical Nation**'.

Letter from David Hume to Lord Hailes, asking for his comments on the draft for Hume's book **Enquiry Concerning the Principles of Morals** *(1753)*

Parliament Close, Edinburgh: this painting of the 1780s by John Kay depicts many well known contemporary Enlightenment figures

'Does Lord Hailes Love Me?'

Dr Samuel Johnson, compiler of the first English dictionary and one of the best known literary figures of the eighteenth century, communicated with **Lord Hailes** through **James Boswell**, a mutual friend. Johnson revised the manuscript of Lord Hailes's most important work, *Annals of Scotland*, for which, according to Boswell, Johnson had nothing but praise:

'*Lord Hailes's Annals of Scotland have not that painted form which is the taste of this age; but it is a book which will always sell, it has such a stability of dates, such a certainty of facts, and such a punctuality of citation. I never before read Scotch history with certainty*'. (Boswell's *Life of Johnson* unabridged edition, Oxford Paperbacks p757).

Letters from Boswell to Lord Hailes, now in the National Library of Scotland, indicate how much the noble lord figured in conversation between Boswell and Johnson: and how often he inspired toasts!

Inner Temple, 23 July 1763: '*Last night [Johnson] and I supt in a room at the Turk's Head Coffee House. He was happy that I had such a friend as you and he said, "an hour's conversation with such a man may be of use to you thro' the whole of life". ... He considers you as a Scholar, as a man of worth and a man of Wit. He drank your health again in a Bumper, and he wished that I would inform you of his opinion of you'.*

London, 1 April 1775: '*I send you eight pages of your Annals revised by Mr Johnson. The red ink in which his notes are written will come off with a wet sponge ... He says will send him some every post ... He says, "Does Lord Hailes love me? I love him." ... Mr Johnson is much pleased with your Annals'.*

Boswell's fulsome praise of Lord Hailes may, however, have been flattery, since he also published a poem satirising Sir David's pedantry. Perhaps he and Johnson were sharing a joke at Lord Hailes's expense!

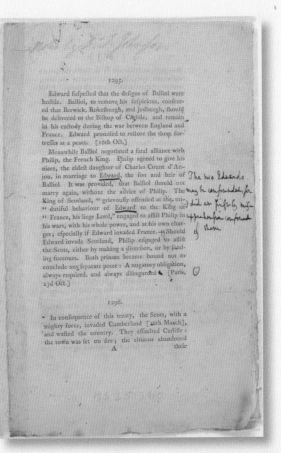

Dr Samuel Johnson,
by George Willison

James Boswell,
by James Barry

*Top: a page from the printer's proof of Lord Hailes's **Annals of Scotland**, with annotations by Dr Samuel Johnson*

Left: watercolour of the Library by Walter Severn, 1869

Miss Christian's diaries record some of the glittering events to which the Library, as the largest room in the house, played host.

'27-28 March 1828: Busy arranging the Library for the Ball … The lamps were put up in the Library in the morning and the Supper Table set out. The Company was mostly assembled by ten and the Dancing went on with spirit, everybody was pleased, and tho' there were many apologies the number was considerably above 100 … The Party was all gone by four, I went to bed at five.'

'6 April 1829: The day of our great Ball … We dressed and the room was prepared. … The whole was thought to go off well tho' I had some things to wish otherwise … The Company I thought was rather too numerous, more than 170. Dancing continued till near four, not in bed till five.'

Hailes Castle

Miss Christian maintained the Library out of respect for her learned family, but also, as a woman, put it to different uses. She made the Library a drawing room, at least in summer. It also became a dining room for very large parties and balls were held here. The handsome cut-glass chandeliers, dating from the mid-eighteenth century and a rare survival in Scotland, are certainly more appropriate to a ballroom than a library.

In 1816, Miss Christian commissioned a family friend, the **Reverend John Thomson** of Duddingston Kirk, to paint two new landscape overdoors, depicting **Hailes Castle** and **Tantallon Castle** in East Lothian, both Dalrymple possessions. In the same year, she paid the staggering sum of 100 guineas (approximately £4,800 in today's money) for the pair of Imari (Japanese export) vases with dragon lids, still in this room.

In 1839 the renowned architect **William Burn** estimated for enclosing the lowest shelves of the Library to form cupboards. Several contain handsome oak parquetry fall-front bureau chests of drawers, with ingeniously concealed bolts. These provided convenient work surfaces, with the necessary papers close to hand in the filing drawers. This collection of early 'office' furniture — possibly associated with the family's administrative role in government — is the largest in Scotland.

Miss Christian's use of the Library as a drawing room was extended by her successors. By the time of the 1873 inventory, this room is known as the '**Drawing Room**', and its transformation was relatively simple. A long suite of sofas and chairs – now, sadly, no longer there – was transferred here from the Drawing Room on the other side of the house, indicating that the old Library had now well and truly assumed this function. However, some other beautiful furniture remains that was brought here to show off during the 'drawing room phase', including the so-called '**Hopetoun cabinet**' from the late seventeenth century.

The polar bearskin hearth rug was a wedding present to Sir Mark and Lady Antonia Dalrymple.

'Dancing continued till near four, not in bed till five'

The suite of two sofas, 16 chairs and four stools that originally graced this room was sold privately in 1928 to a Glasgow bidder, because the Newhailes trustees feared for its security: it is probably now in the United States. Lord Hailes had bought the suite at a sale of furniture from an aunt's house in Greek Street, London, in the 1760s. We can appreciate from this photograph of the sofa the quality of the upholstery that takes up the recurring shell theme at Newhailes.

Bottom: Sir Mark as a baby on one of the tapestry chairs

Clockwise from top: Library chandelier; wall lamp; Chinese ceramic bowl detail; chimneypiece detail

The diaries of Miss Christian record the efforts needed to maintain the condition of the collection:

'18 June 1815: It rained heavily: the water poured through the unfinished Roof and we were forced to take down one side of the Books in the Library.'

'17 December 1816: A man from the Bookbinders examined my Books and found them not in a good state and vigorous measures necessary to prevent the worm from spreading.'

Extensive damage by bookworm was again discovered in 1850, when the paper that had covered the shelves for several years, to prevent possible harm by tenants, was removed.

At the National Library of Scotland, the Newhailes book collection has been kept in secure and environmentally controlled conditions. In accordance with the wishes of the Newhailes trustees and the Heritage Lottery Fund, The National Trust for Scotland is currently in negotiation with the National Library to return many of these books to this, their original home.

A Rich Resource

The books originally in this Library were largely acquired by **Lord Hailes**, adding to the collection of his grandfather, **Sir David Dalrymple**. Many of them, including works by **Johnson** and **Boswell**, were sold by Sotheby's in 1937. After the death of **Sir Mark Dalrymple** in 1971, the remaining 7,000 volumes were passed in lieu of death duty into the care of the National Library of Scotland in Edinburgh, whose catalogue describes them as *'the most important contemporary collection to survive from the period of the Scottish Enlightenment'.*

The collection tells us a lot about the interests of Lord Hailes: it is strongest in history and biography (1,800 volumes); classical and modern literature (2,500); law, politics and economics (around 1,000) and theology (750). Notable items include the rare **Ode on a Distant Prospect of Eton College (1747)**, the poet **Thomas Gray's** first publication, and magnificent architectural folios such as **Palladio's Venice (1616)**. Papers include letters between Lord Hailes and famous contemporaries such as **David Hume**; and charts by Lord Hailes's brother **Alexander**, the first hydrographer to the Admiralty, together with his East Indies nautical memoirs.

Below: view of Library looking south-east
Left: writing desk details
Background: collage of frontispieces from books in the Newhailes collection, now in the National Library of Scotland

The China Closet

When the weather was cold and it was impossible to heat the huge Library properly, this compact, cosy room, with its corner fireplace and door with draught-proof hinge, was the perfect place to work. It is not surprising that, in Scotland, such closets were considered integral components of libraries. **Sir James Dalrymple** gave this tiny room an exotic flavour by commissioning the carving of Chinoiserie-inspired panels and grotesque oriental heads on the elaborate doorcases. The 1790s inventory records that these panels were covered with the same patterned Indian silk as the window curtains. Unfortunately, this has at some stage been removed with a razor blade, but traces still remain at the back of the panels.

Miss Christian gave this room a new purpose as a **China Closet** — perhaps to replace the deteriorating pale silk wall panels and to alleviate the gloom of the olive-green paint applied in 1739. In 1822 she added the little pillared shelves, made of oak to match the Library. Early in that year, she records in her diary: '*China partly put up in the China Closet, which looked beautiful. In shops getting Crimson Cloth and Silks for China Closet*.' The rich effect is increased by the huge number of brackets added to display individual teacups and saucers.

Some of the china retains old metal and rivet repairs — a few, no doubt, incurred by the visit of a clumsy guest, tartly recalled by Miss Christian in her diary entry of 11 July 1825: '*Mr Inglis here, he broke Cups & Saucers in the China Closet*.'

The closet evidently did not receive regular attention from the owners or tenants of the house after Miss Christian's death. In October 1902, Alice Mary writes to her father, Sir Charles Dalrymple, about her overhaul of the collection: '*Wattie and I have been washing all the china and arranging it in order today in the china room. It was fearfully dirty and we have picked out the things which need mending. She rather hesitated at first, but when she saw I was so keen, she warmed up! ... One could hardly see the patterns for the dust!*'

'China partly put up in the China Closet, which looked beautiful.

In shops getting Crimson Cloth and Silks for China Closet.'

Most of the china you see here now must have been collected by Miss Christian's grandmother, Lady Christian, and illustrates the history of Western porcelain. Most is of standard Chinese export type, but there are some examples of Meissen, the first European imitations of oriental wares, and a significant amount of Japanese porcelain. The Sienese majolica plates on the chimney-breast are unusual, and were possibly brought back from Italy along with the Library chimneypiece. But the rarest and most surprising items are the 20 pieces from the short-lived porcelain factory established locally by William Littler at West Pans, near Musselburgh, in 1764.

Below (top to bottom): Persian
figurehead fireplace detail (Winter
Sitting Room); lion head fireplace
detail (Dining Room); ribbon
knotwork (Winter Sitting Room)

Opposite page: view from the Dining
Room

The Great Apartment

The visitor to Newhailes now crosses the entrance hall again to the Great Apartment, added by **Sir James** and **Lady Christian Dalrymple** between 1728 and 1733 to balance his father's Library Wing at the west end of the house. The five rooms making up the Apartment were designed for the entertainment and accommodation of guests.

The survival in a Scottish house of a Great Apartment as intact as this is exceptional. It follows the format, well established by the late seventeenth century, of a long chain of connected rooms, ending in a back stair. At Newhailes, this was a considerable challenge to the unknown architect, who had to fit all this into a space no bigger than the west wing of the house, and restrict the height of the rooms to match those in Smith's relatively modest original villa.

In Scotland the first room in the sequence, the great dining room, was always the largest — perhaps to allow room for all the servants waiting at table to move around. Next came the withdrawing room, usually square, where the company would withdraw after their formal dinner and which would be furnished for the service of tea. This room also served as an ante-chamber to the best bedroom — the one where the most important guest slept.

Beyond this, and usually connected with the back stair, was a dressing room. This could be surprisingly grand, as an illustrious guest might receive intimate friends here while the finishing touches were added to his or her hair and formal dress.

Together, these rooms formed one of the most elaborately decorated and carefully thought-out rococo interiors in Scotland. The distinctive ribbon-and-flower mouldings of the decorative carver, **William Strachan**, can also be seen at Hopetoun House (near Edinburgh), and at two National Trust for Scotland properties, House of Dun (near Montrose) and Haddo House (Aberdeenshire), but the overall effect is unique to Newhailes. At Hopetoun and Dun the '**great apartments**' were much changed in the nineteenth century, when many dining rooms were converted into drawing rooms, new dining rooms formed out of the old withdrawing rooms and bedrooms knocked together. At Newhailes, the Library in the opposite wing became the drawing room, and the Great Apartment was left undisturbed, so it has survived in its eighteenth-century form.

The rooms are also exceptional for the quality of their fireplaces, bought in London. As a Member of Parliament for Haddington, and frequently attending at Westminster, Sir James would have been familiar with London fashions, and seems to have been aware of the work of **William Kent**, Britain's pioneer interior decorator. Sir James's wife Lady Christian probably contributed to the design: we know from the 1790s inventory that she made carpets for three of the rooms.

The Dining Room

A very large dining room was considered essential for entertaining at the time of **Sir James** and **Lady Christian**. They responded imaginatively to the challenge of creating a sufficiently imposing room within the scale of Smith's original villa: they had the floor lowered to gain maximum height, and the gable wall demolished so that the room could extend into the new wing. A screen of Ionic columns replaced this wall, creating an area where servants could prepare everything they needed to serve food at the table.

The impressive chimneypiece was made by the celebrated London sculptor **Henry Cheere**. The Dalrymples' alterations meant that guests entered this newly extended space with the fireplace behind them – the wrong place for the traditional focus of a room. They resolved this by placing a huge plate of mirror glass on the opposite wall to reflect the fireplace. This magnificent mirror is built up from glitteringly bevelled panes held in place by brass strips, as in the famous Hall of Mirrors at Versailles.

Sir James and Lady Christian also approached the decoration of the room in a very original way. Instead of commissioning the conventional overdoor paintings depicting idealised Italianate landscapes – as in other rooms at Newhailes – the Dalrymples ordered paintings of their own property from the Dutch artist **Isaac Vogelsang**. These four views – of which one is reproduced below – show different aspects of the house in its remarkable coastal setting in the shadow of Arthur's Seat: the sketchy figures may be the Dalrymple family.

This letter from Henry Cheere to Sir James Dalrymple, dated 6 September, 1739, suggests that his noble patron had asked Cheere to execute some last-minute alterations to the chimneypiece. He protests that the work is so far advanced that: '*it cannot without a great deal of expense be altered*'. We do not know whether his appeal to Sir James's pocket prevailed.

The Drawing Room (Winter Sitting Room)

This room was one of the most innovative in the house. Athough its position is that of the traditional '**withdrawing room**', it breaks with custom in that it is rectangular rather than square, giving it an importance similar to that of the dining room. The new shape allows for a classically balanced arrangement of triple windows, with magnificent pier glasses in between, decorated with massive sculpted shells. The bases of their frames were designed to hold candle-branches at night: imagine the brilliant effect of the light reflected in the mirrors and the bright gilding.

The opposite wall is long enough to accommodate a pair of sofas and a spectacular chimneypiece, one of three supplied by the sculptor **Henry Cheere** and surely one of the most ambitious of the early eighteenth century in Scotland. It is carved from expensive pure white statuary marble, which was usually reserved for figurative sculpture. The bearded, turbanned figures depict Persians. The frieze is a dense festoon of exquisitely carved, realistically observed blooms, a feminine motif that indicates this room was intended for the ladies, as a balance to the Dining Room, the province of the gentlemen.

Although still crammed with splendid things, the room is now only a shadow of its former glory. **A watercolour of 1858** by Charles Vaughan (left) shows that, at a time when wallpaper was usually confined to panels, every wall in this room was once covered with elaborate Chinese wallpaper. This bore a panoramic landscape design running all the way round the room, rather than repetitions of a pattern. The Shands took down the wallpaper to display their collection of modern paintings. When the Dalrymples resumed occupation of the house, they replaced the Shands' paintings with a run of family portraits, most of which remain here.

Note the gilded eagles flying into the room over each window — they probably originally held curtain rods in their talons.

In 2002 the Trust returned the fine tapestry fire-screen to this room, its original home (it had been used in the Library). Its blue background would have matched the 'blue damask curtains' listed in the 1790s inventory, and it serves to suggest the splendour of this room's original furnishings.

The costly decoration of the room required protection from light — still very necessary today, despite the loss of the Chinese wallpaper. The joiners who built the original window frames included slots for roller blinds, with the mechanism concealed in the cavities at the top of the windows. One of these original blinds has survived. The red blinds here now are replicas of those installed in the nineteenth century.

Opposite page: the Drawing Room, photographed as it was in 1996

The Secret of the Lacquer Chest

The bed here now is not the original 'best bed'. When the Trust acquired Newhailes, all that remained of the best bed was an indication of its site — the break in the dado and the plain panelling immediately opposite the window, and a blank panel opposite the fireplace. There were also lines of nailing where the headcloth of the bed had been secured to the wall, and screw holes for the brackets of a wooden canopy. We also knew that the 1790s inventory mentioned '*an India embroidered bed lined with blue silk; a coverlet the same lin'd with white stuff; a window curtain the same lined with white silk; a piece of hanging the same*'. In 1998, in true fairytale fashion, the key was found to a lacquer chest in the Vestibule which, when opened, revealed a set of embroidered Chinese white silk bed hangings with blue fringes, carefully repaired and excellently preserved. In January 2002, the bed was partially assembled on a temporary frame, and this photograph (right) taken as a record.

The differential fading of the hangings may indicate that the bed was dismantled gradually. We know that the wall panel and headcloth were still *in situ* in 1873, when the inventory lists them as '*2 tapestry panels on wall*', but the bed and the rest of the hangings had probably been put away with the beginning of the Shands' tenancy. This is why many of the hangings have survived so well, in contrast to the matching embroidered Chinese silk on the firescreen, now in almost unrecognisable shreds because of the destructive effects of light.

The Best Bedroom

This was where the most important guest slept. The chimneypiece, again in pure white statuary marble, is the third of those supplied by **Henry Cheere**. It follows a design by **Inigo Jones**, the renowned English architect and designer of the early eighteenth century. Above it is a giltwood mirror embellished with carved shells and fishscales. The single window looks larger than it is because of the flanking plates of bevelled glass. Its very slim early nineteenth-century iron sashes allowed an unrestricted view of the Flower Garden underneath the window.

This was **Sir Charles Dalrymple's** bedroom before the house was let to the Shands, and when he lived here again as a widower. In the twentieth century, **Sir Mark** and **Lady Antonia** slept here when they were first married, and moved the grander pieces of furniture to other less used parts of the house.

Left, top: chimneypiece detail
Bottom: detail of wooden statuette

The Dressing Room

The rich decoration of the Dressing Room shows that it was designated for the principal guest. The corner fireplace has a cascade of cup-and-saucer stands which were possibly emptied by **Miss Christian** when she created her China Closet on the other side of the house. Like all the principal rooms at Newhailes, it retains its original grate. It is not clear why only three panels have been papered with the elaborately painted Chinese wallpaper – perhaps the material was salvaged from the Drawing Room.

The painting of a man's head, probably by **Medina**, in an octagonal frame, and the Italian oval marble panel, depicting the Holy Family with St John the Baptist and St Anne, came from the collection of Sir James Dalrymple's brother.

The 1790s inventory gives details of the key feature once here: *'a toilet table & dressing glass; a Worked Muslin toilet & vail, & a blew gauze to throw over it. A Japan tray, 12 boxes & an agate box.'* The room also contained *'a bason stand, China bason & China bottle'* and a *'Japan close stool [portable toilet].'*

Visitors now leave by the servants' entrance – a narrow, concealed floor-to-ceiling door – and take the spiral service stair to the first-floor bedrooms. The Dalrymples and their guests would probably have used Smith's original wrought-iron main staircase.

Below: Chinese wallpaper detail

Bottom: panelling with mid-seventeenth-century Italian marble relief

The Green Bedroom

This family bedchamber — where the paint colour is now, perhaps, more aptly
described as 'black' than 'green' — was occupied by **Sir James** and **Lady Christian**
themselves, and was the most highly decorated bedroom in the house.

The Dalrymples' desire to gain as much height as possible for their great reception
rooms, immediately below, means that the rooms up here burrow into the roof space,
leaving no room for attics above. In the mid-nineteenth century the Dressing Room
next door became an extra bedroom, with a new passageway cutting into the bed
alcove space here. The shrunken alcove was turned into a wardrobe, with imitation
gilded leather door panels. Even in its mutilated form this alcove — together with
its companion in the Alcove Bedroom — is a very rare survivor. To the Victorians,
obsessed with improving sanitation and ventilation, bed alcoves were positively
unhealthy, and were usually broken down to create larger rooms. The brass and iron
bedsteads at Newhailes, probably installed by the **Shands**, were also a Victorian
innovation: it was believed that, unlike wooden beds, they did not harbour bugs.

A special feature of this room is its large unpanelled expanses, planned from the
outset to display wallpaper. The handsome polychrome imitation leather papers on the
alcove wardrobe door were installed for the Shands and may be French. But the most
remarkable architectural feature is the extraordinary recess with shaped shelves with
stacked pigeon-holes at each end. The shelves can be concealed with a panel, painted to
match the wall decoration, and which fits into a specially created recess in the passage
to the **Dressing Room**. There is nothing like this in any other Scottish country house,
and it is probable that Lady Christian had them built to display her china collection.

All the hearth-slabs on this floor retain beautiful feather-banded parquetry
surrounds, made from contrasting woods. Above the fireplace hangs, appropriately,
a portrait of **Lady Christian** by **Ramsay**, dated 1744. In the alcove is a handsome
pair of portraits of Sir James Dalrymple's sister **Janet**, by Ramsay, and her husband
General James St Clair, by **Jean Marc Nattier**, both painted in 1749.

The painted decoration gives the final remarkable distinction to this elaborate room.
The survival of such decoration is unique in Scotland, though some of the finer detail
has been obscured by a darkened coat of varnish. Note the painted busts over the
entrance door and the door to the Dressing Room: one has a plinth in shaped glass, a
clever way of allowing borrowed light through to the entrance passage.

The Dalrymples enlivened the first-floor passage by hanging here paintings by members of the family. From this passage there are commanding views over the parkland to the River Forth.

The Yellow Room

This was **Lady Christian's** dressing room, her private retreat, and decorated with a richness suitable to her status as daughter of the Earl of Haddington. Its walls were hung with blue silk, now only visible in two long panels. The rest is concealed underneath glazed chintz, which was presumably put up for protection when the Shands rented the house. The citron-colour paintwork dates from the Shands' redecoration. Lord Shand suggested installing a bath in this room but Charles Dalrymple, not surprisingly, objected, as it would have destroyed the original gilding, which has been preserved.

The Alcove Bedroom

The alcove bedchamber is the most evocative at Newhailes, because it is the least altered. It was probably the Dalrymples' principal guest apartment after the Best Bedroom on the floor below. **Sir David Hunter Blair**, Sir Charles Dalrymple's brother-in-law, recalled sleeping in this room in his memoirs, published in 1936: '*I went out for a night to Newhailes... It was nice to occupy once again the charming "alcove" room with its recessed bed (very Scottish), old embroidered hangings, lovely slim doors, and everywhere egg-and-tongue and bead-and-reel mouldings on a dim green ground*'.

The 1790s inventory refers to a '*chest of drawers with a marble top*'. This may refer to the ormolu-mounted commode that is still here, of French Régence (early rococo) design: it is very rare for a piece of French furniture to have remained in the same place in a British room for so long, as this has.

Opposite page: the Alcove Bedroom photographed in 1996. Inset (left to right) chair detail, water jug and bowl, detail from ormolu-mounted commode, detail of William Morris 'pomegranate' wallpaper design

a 'green lung' for local people

and a place where visitors can

find peace to enjoy wildlife

An Oasis of Wildlife

Today, Newhailes is surrounded by urban encroachment. Despite **Miss Christian's** legal safeguards against her heirs removing trees at Newhailes, many beech, elm, ash, sycamore, willow and lime trees were sold after her death. But it still contains one of the largest woodlands in the Edinburgh area which, together with its open parkland, allow for a surprisingly wide variety of wildlife on an estate within a few miles of the centre of Scotland's capital city. Newhailes plays an important role as a 'corridor' allowing animals and plants to move between other green areas within Edinburgh and beyond into the wider countryside. It is also a '**green lung**' for local people and a place where visitors can find peace to enjoy wildlife without the distractions of the city.

The woodland here has changed with time. The original planting design has gradually been transformed by changing fashions in forestry and by the processes of nature. Woodland management in the past has left few trees of any great age – we believe there was a major felling programme around the time of World War I. The most ancient trees are those close to the house, evidently spared because they were regarded as aesthetically important. Yews, holm oaks and sweet chestnuts still remain, alongside beech, lime, sycamore (supplanting the elms infected by Dutch elm disease), holly, larch and ash, with its striking jet-black buds. Scrub species, such as hawthorn, elder and the introduced lilac, have grown thickly along Ladies' Walk and in many areas of the woodlands, providing cover and food for the multitude of birds that visit and breed on the estate. In places, ivy carpets the woodland floor and climbs up trees, giving vital sustenance and cover to wildlife and contributing to the natural evolution of the woodland.

Beneath the tree canopy, native woodland plants such as wood avens (often known as herb bennet), wood anemone, dog violet and wood sorrel thrive, together with later introductions such as hybrid bluebell, star-of-Bethlehem and snowdrop. Their bright, fresh colours combine with the chorus of birdsong to herald the arrival of spring. Newhailes supports over 60 different species of bird, many of which breed here. Blue, great and coal tits, chaffinches, chiffchaffs and song thrushes can be seen flitting around the branches, the wood edges and the parkland.

Nearer the house, the parkland and lawns also hold much wildlife interest. The Trust's low-intensity management regime within the parks has encouraged the development of large areas of open grassland that were originally pasture and then arable land. These are now home to the grey partridge – locally uncommon – and are used by large flocks of curlew coming off the Firth of Forth in winter. The parklands are also botanically diverse, supporting species such as common poppy, goat's-beard and tansy. The dense grass makes a good habitat for field voles and mice, which in turn attract kestrel and tawny owl to hunt and breed within the estate. Foxes, stoats, weasels, bats and shrews live here and in the woodland, as do a great variety of invertebrates, including over 180 species of moth and 11 species of butterfly. Occasionally, otters may be seen.

The Trust carefully records the wildlife at Newhailes and supports the work of visiting natural historians. A new species of fungus – *Ascozonus monascus* – was recently discovered on the front apron outside the house: it makes its home on rabbit droppings.

Our overall management of the estate takes full account of the wildlife here, though sometimes valuable habitats have to be removed in order to conserve historical features of national importance. The Trust plans to manage the wider expanses of the parkland in a way that will bring in much more wildlife, and that will also contribute to the unique ambience of the place.

Below: three stages in the repair of the external handrail and newel post

Opposite page (main image): front elevation of house under survey

Inset: front elevation covered in scaffolding

The Conservation of Newhailes

The Trust's conservation policy for Newhailes has been to do **as much as necessary** to stabilise the condition of the buildings and the estate and prevent further deterioration, but **as little as possible**, so that the mellow character and ambience is protected. The project has been a true challenge because, while leaving everything as '**undisturbed**' as possible, the Trust still had to address the continuing deterioration of the house, environmental conditions appropriate to the collections, public safety, and the need for essential accommodation for staff and visitors.

Immediately after acquiring Newhailes in 1997, the Trust undertook historical research and survey work into its origins, development and significance, the better to inform our conservation plan. The specialist survey work included such diverse elements as landfill and topographic reports, glazing and paintwork analysis, and surveys on collections such as the clocks and ceramics.

Meanwhile, essential repairs were carried out that could not wait. These included the installation of a fire main to service the estate; emergency stabilisation of the boundary walls and the doocot, which is currently hidden under a temporary roof until further conservation work can proceed; and urgent repairs to the Stable Block and Gate Lodge.

We discovered that parts of the external render (plastering) of the house dated back to the late seventeenth century, and we tried to keep as much of this as possible. Our research showed that the render was originally lined out to imitate ashlar stonework (hewn blocks of squared stone), and then finished in a coat of limewash which was over-painted in oil paint to emphasise the 'ashlar' joints.

Plate glass replaced the original smaller glazing panes on the principal floor as part of the 1873 alterations to the house. In line with our conservation philosophy, the Trust decided to respect this significant change to the house. All the existing glass, including cracked panes, was retained wherever possible, and repaired. Where new glass was necessary, the Trust sourced matching replacements.

Our works to the outside of the house included the dismantling and reassembling of the main staircase to the entrance door, to make it safe. Both the balusters and the timber handrail fitted in 1873 have been retained without replacing missing sections, except where these compromised safety.

The roof over the kitchen court to the west of the house was missing when the Trust acquired the property and, as no evidence of its original appearance has come to light, a simple glazed structure has been provided to prevent further deterioration.

the Trust has strived to retain
all existing surface textures